TITLE I
HOLMES JR HIGH
2001-02

# Earth watch

Written by
**DAVID BURNIE**
Consultant
DR PHILIP WHITFIELD

A Dorling Kindersley Book

**Dorling DK Kindersley**

LONDON, NEW YORK, SYDNEY, DELHI,
PARIS, MUNICH, and JOHANNESBURG

**Project Editor** Kitty Blount
**Art Editor** Mark Regardsoe
**Senior Editor** Fran Jones
**Managing Editor** Sue Grabham
**Senior Managing Art Editor** Julia Harris
**Picture Researchers** Christine Rista, Amanda Russell
**Production** Kate Oliver and Chris Avgherinos
**DTP Designer** Andrew O'Brien
**US Editor** Chuck Wills

First American edition 2001
01 02 03 04 05 10 9 8 7 6 5 4 3 2

Published in the United States by
Dorling Kindersley Publishing, Inc.
95 Madison Avenue
New York, New York 10016

Library of Congress Cataloging-in-Publication Data

Burnie, David.
   Make a difference. Earthwatch / written by David Burnie ; consultant,
Philip Whitfield.
   p. cm.
   ISBN 0-7894-6895-6
   1. Environmental sciences--Juvenile literature. 2. Earth--Environmental
aspects--Juvenile literature. [1. Environmental sciences. 2. Environmental
protection.]

   GE115 .B87 2001
   333.7--dc21

00-043014

Reproduced by Colourscan, Singapore
Printed and bound by L.E.G.O., Italy

See our complete catalog at
**www.dk.com**

# Contents

# Introduction

Today is an exciting
time to be living on planet Earth.
Almost every week, there are new breakthroughs
in technology that allow us to achieve the unthinkable. Thanks to
satellites and computers, we can track storms as they move across
the globe. High-powered cameras can pick out almost any feature
on the Earth's surface – from fields and forests to houses and roads
– and tiny radio transmitters can track individual animals, telling
us exactly where they go and how they behave. With information
like this at our fingertips, we know more about our planet
than ever before.

What all this information tells us is that the world is more
complicated than most of us could ever imagine. Almost
everything on it, whether it lives on the land or in the sea,
is connected in some way. This means that the whole
planet is our home, and whatever we do can also
have an impact on things that live far away.

It also tells us that our planet is not as healthy
as it could be. Much of it is affected by
pollution, and by the growing mountain of
items that we throw away. At the same
time, the human population is rising
fast, which means we are taking up
more and more space. As a result,
Earth's natural habitats are

being changed or destroyed, making it harder for plants and animals to find room for themselves. This book will help you understand the problems that face the natural world. You will discover why scientists are worried about the world becoming warmer and how organic farming can save the soil.

The good news about the environment is that many of the world's problems – such as water pollution – are now being tackled in a determined way. But we still have a long way to go. On some of the main issues, such as global warming or growing food, experts do not always agree on the problems or what should be done. In this book, you will find both sides of the argument provide a clear picture of what is at stake.

&&"Means must be found to tackle the root causes of environmental problems...""

UNITED NATIONS ENVIRONMENT PROGRAM, EARTHSCAN 2000

Because the Earth is so big, it is easy to feel there is nothing we can do to help. But individuals can make a difference. In this book, there are suggestions for ways you can play an active role, and experiments to provide first-hand experience of some of the scientific issues. Day in the Life journals describe the work of experts in the field, while letters from young people around the world reveal their concerns about the environment. If we act now, we can all help to safeguard the future of the planet.

# BEAUTIFUL
## PLANET

A HUGE VARIETY OF PLANTS AND ANIMALS LIVE ON EARTH. THEY NEED CLEAN AIR AND FRESH WATER TO SURVIVE. Over the last 100 years, advances in technology have led us to fill the atmosphere with harmful gases and pollute the rivers and oceans. Now it is up to us to take care of the rich and vibrant home we share.

> **"** We have inherited a planet of exquisite beauty. It is the gift of four billion years of evolution. We need to regain our ancient feeling for the Earth as an organism and to revere it again. **"**

**JAMES LOVELOCK**
**SCIENTIST AND ENVIRONMENTALIST**

Disappearing into thick forest, a rainbow signals the end of a downpour on the Caribbean island of St. Lucia (main picture). Much of St. Lucia's tree cover is still intact, but elsewhere in the world, natural forests are vanishing fast. In British Columbia (inset), this giant paper mill uses up more than a million tons of wood every year.

# Living world

**N**o matter where you go on Earth, you are never far from other living things. Some of them are far bigger and will live far longer than you, but many are so tiny that you could hold millions of them in your hand. Despite their differences, they all depend on each other for survival. Together, they form a delicately balanced web of life. Today, that web of life is under threat for various reasons, such as increased levels of pollution. As caretakers of the planet, we need to find out where these threats come from, and what can be done to reduce their impact.

## Soaking up the Sun

Plants are the key to life on Earth because they provide food for other living things. These swamp cypresses are doing just that, by absorbing energy from sunlight and converting it into food. Trees and other plants also release oxygen into the air, making the atmosphere fit to breathe. Without oxygen, few living things could survive.

## Eaters and eaten

There are many different types of animals on Earth, and all of them have to eat to survive. This deer will get its energy by grazing on plants. Many animals get their energy in a different way – by eating each other.

**Good food**
Deer feed on tree leaves. But wolves hunt and eat deer to stay alive.

**Living skin**
Compared to the entire Earth, the area where life is found – the biosphere – is like a thin skin on the surface of the planet.

## A shared home

The biosphere is a layer of life that surrounds the whole of the Earth. It extends from the upper atmosphere to well below the surface of the ground and the oceans. This layer contains the natural homes, or habitats, of all living things. Unlike humans, other creatures are often very particular about where they live. For example, deer almost always inhabit forests, while the brittlestar's home is on the seabed.

# A slice of life

Here is a slice through part of the biosphere, together with some of its inhabitants. Plants need light to grow, so they always live out in the open. Animals and microbes – very small living things such as bacteria – are different. They get their energy from food, or sometimes from their surroundings. This means that they can live in a wider range of habitats, including ones that are permanently dark.

**Pollen grains**
This dustlike substance is produced by flowers, and enables them to make seeds. Pollen is often spread by the wind, and it can be blown many miles into the air.

**Bald eagle**
Eagles live in wide open places such as mountainsides and moorlands. They need this kind of habitat because they soar up high, and find their prey from the air.

There may be **more than 30 million** different kinds of **living things** on Earth

**Foxglove**
Foxgloves live under trees, and also in woodland glades. This habitat gives them shelter from the wind and the cold.

**Ballan wrasse**
Wrasses live among rocks and seaweed close to the coast. Like most coastal fish, they stick to this habitat and never venture into deeper water.

**Brittlestar**
These spidery starfish live on the seabed, often in water more than 3,300 ft (1,000 m) deep. Unlike the wrasse, they can survive in complete darkness, where no plants can grow.

Unless we **act** now, a quarter of all **species** on **Earth** may be **lost** in the next **30 years**

**Rock bacteria**
Some bacteria can survive in rock more than 1.25 miles (2 km) underground. They do not depend on energy from the Sun.

> **"The global average temperature will be at least 1.8°F (1°C) warmer by the year 2030."**
>
> INTER-GOVERNMENTAL PANEL
> ON CLIMATE CHANGE 1990

## Natural climate change

About 20,000 years ago – near the end of the last Ice Age – much of the northern hemisphere was covered by ice. In the area around New York City, the ice was hundreds of feet thick. The ice retreated 15,000 years ago, leaving windswept tundra. By about 7,500 years ago, the climate became warmer still, and the tundra turned into forest. These changes were part of a natural cycle that will probably repeat itself – when, nobody knows.

Ice Age: 20,000 years ago      Tundra: 15,000 years ago

# *Changing* CLIMATES

Global warming could cause **sea** levels to rise by **39 in** (100 cm) in the **21st century**

Ever since life first appeared on Earth, it has had to cope with changes in climate. Climatologists have several theories about why these natural changes happen, but most of them agree about one thing: our planet is now warming up extremely fast, and this time humans have caused much of the change. The Sun warms the Earth and certain gases, such as carbon dioxide, trap the heat in the atmosphere. This occurs naturally and is called the greenhouse effect. Burning oil, coal, or gas produces extra carbon dioxide, which steps up the greenhouse effect and overheats our planet.

## Dry times

People can affect the climate in many ways. In dry places like the Namib desert, overgrazing by animals strips away the ground's plant cover. Without plants, it is harder for the soil to hold water, and the ground gets hotter in the day. The result is drier air and less rainfall – two things that can turn the land into desert.

Forest: 7,500 years ago

New York City today

## Adapt or die

Natural climate changes usually happen slowly, so plants and animals can adapt. Today's global warming is different because it is happening much more quickly. This rapid warming could wipe out many species that cannot adapt in time.

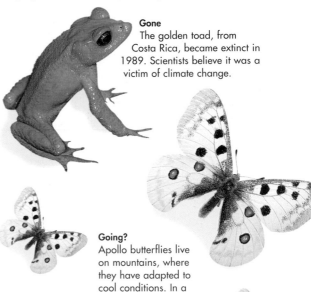

**Gone**
The golden toad, from Costa Rica, became extinct in 1989. Scientists believe it was a victim of climate change.

**Going?**
Apollo butterflies live on mountains, where they have adapted to cool conditions. In a warming world, they will have to move higher up to survive.

## Signs of change

In Britain, biologists have discovered that spring is starting earlier each year – almost certainly because of global warming. Some trees now come into leaf 10 days sooner than they used to 40 years ago. Birds are also laying their eggs earlier in the year.

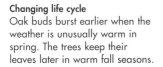

**Changing life cycle**
Oak buds burst earlier when the weather is unusually warm in spring. The trees keep their leaves later in warm fall seasons.

**Early families**
Chaffinches lay their eggs earlier as spring arrives sooner.

## Rising sea levels

A dramatic result of global warming is the melting of the polar icecaps. As temperatures increase, polar glaciers carry more ice from land into the sea. When this ice melts, the sea level rises. Within the next 100 years, low-lying islands, such as the Maldives, and coastal cities are in danger of being engulfed by the sea.

## THE GREENHOUSE EFFECT

*EXPERIMENT*

**You will need:** 2 small jars, 1 large, clear glass or plastic bowl, some water, and plenty of sunshine!

**1 HALF FILL EACH** jar with water. Put the jars in the Sun, either outdoors or indoors next to an open window. Put the clear bowl upside down over one of the jars. Leave for one hour.

Heat trapped inside bowl

**2 REMOVE THE BOWL.** Dip your finger in each jar to compare the temperatures of the water inside. The water in the jar covered by the bowl will be warmer than the water in the other one.

**This shows that:** the bowl acts like a heat trap, letting light energy in, but preventing infrared (heat) energy from getting out. Carbon dioxide and other gases do the same thing in the atmosphere, causing the Earth to warm up.

**GLACIOLOGIST**
DAVID VAUGHAN

DAVID VAUGHAN SPENDS MOST OF HIS TIME BEHIND A COMPUTER IN THE BRITISH ANTARCTIC SURVEY OFFICES IN CAMBRIDGE. BUT EVERY THREE YEARS HE SWAPS his desk for a snowmobile and travels to the icy waters at the bottom of the world – Antarctica. For three months he lives in a tent collecting information about the Antarctic ice sheet.

# A day in the life of a
# GLACIOLOGIST

## The data gathered helps us to understand how the Earth's changing climate may affect the Antarctic ice cap.

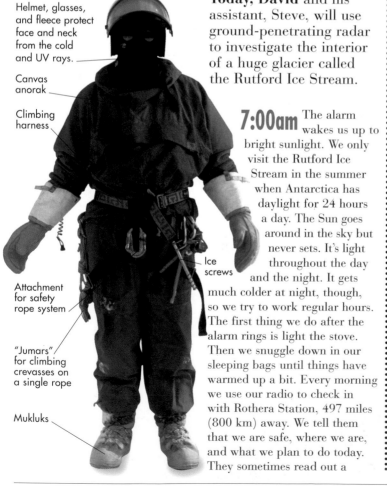

Helmet, glasses, and fleece protect face and neck from the cold and UV rays.

Canvas anorak

Climbing harness

Ice screws

Attachment for safety rope system

"Jumars" for climbing crevasses on a single rope

Mukluks

**Today, David** and his assistant, Steve, will use ground-penetrating radar to investigate the interior of a huge glacier called the Rutford Ice Stream.

**7:00am** The alarm wakes us up to bright sunlight. We only visit the Rutford Ice Stream in the summer when Antarctica has daylight for 24 hours a day. The Sun goes around in the sky but never sets. It's light throughout the day and the night. It gets much colder at night, though, so we try to work regular hours. The first thing we do after the alarm rings is light the stove. Then we snuggle down in our sleeping bags until things have warmed up a bit. Every morning we use our radio to check in with Rothera Station, 497 miles (800 km) away. We tell them that we are safe, where we are, and what we plan to do today. They sometimes read out a

message for us from home. Still in our sleeping bags, we make tea and oatmeal for breakfast.

**8:00am** Time to get out of bed and get dressed for a day outside in temperatures of -4°F (-20°C). We start with a layer of thermal underwear, two layers of fleece, a padded jacket for warmth, and then a canvas anorak to keep out the wind. Our specially warm boots are called mukluks. Today these are made for the Canadian Army, but they are an adaptation of an old Inuit design. Finally, we put on cowls,

**Tracking the ice's movements**
David places a pole in the ice with a Global Positioning System (GPS) antenna attached to it. He is recording his exact position.

which are hats that protect our heads from UV rays, gloves, sunglasses, and plenty of sunscreen.

**8:30am** We emerge from the tent. Steve uncovers the snowmobile and packs a sled with emergency survival equipment. I mount the ground-penetrating radar equipment on another sled. Then I take a GPS reading of our exact position.

GPS antenna

**Same place next year?**
The pole is left in the ice for a year. If the ice has moved, the pole will have moved with it.

Cowl

> **"** Tiredness is the biggest enemy – if you allow yourself to get tired, you'll start making mistakes and that can be dangerous. **"**

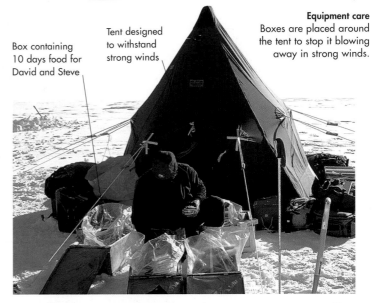

Box containing 10 days food for David and Steve

Tent designed to withstand strong winds

**Equipment care**
Boxes are placed around the tent to stop it blowing away in strong winds.

**Radar**
Ground-penetrating radar is attached to sledge.

**9:00am** We leave camp. Steve drives the snowmobile, towing the two sleds, one carrying emergency equipment and the other the radar system and me. My job is to monitor the equipment and make sure the data is of good quality. We have a code of hand signals that I use to tell Steve to speed up, slow down, or stop. As we travel across the ice cap, the radar builds up a picture of the interior of the ice. We can see the layers in the snow corresponding to specific storms and seasons. This helps us to interpret how old the ice is. We can also see crevasses or cracks buried in the ice. Crevasses are formed when the forces in the ice become too great. The radar data helps me to understand what controls the flow of the Rutford Ice Stream and how this could change in the future.

**1:00pm** We stop for lunch. Because of the cold, we burn a lot of calories and have to eat a lot. We rest and drink a flask of coffee, eat some sardines from a can, and munch on chocolate for energy.

**1:30pm** Back to work – it's too cold to sit around for long! This time I drive the snowmobile. Swapping jobs helps us to stay alert and fight off tiredness.

**7:00pm** We return to camp. While I make a backup of the data we have collected, Steve cooks dinner in the tent. Most of the data we collect is stored on computers that are specially designed for use in the cold. Every evening I copy all the data onto magnetic tapes, and I make copies of my notebooks by hand, in case I happen to lose one of the tapes.

Oats

Sardines

Chocolate

Thermos flask

**8:30pm** We eat dinner and prepare for bed. The last thing we do before going to bed is to cut some snow blocks and store them at the door of the tent. That way we have snow handy to melt into water for our early morning cup of tea tomorrow.

**Ice over the land**
The Rutford Ice Stream is like a giant conveyor belt of ice, more than 186 miles (300 km) long, 25 miles (40 km) wide, and 4,922 feet (1,500 m) thick.

PACIFIC OCEAN

Antarctic Peninsula

WEDDELL SEA

ANTARCTICA

Rutford Ice Stream

ATLANTIC OCEAN

**Ice in the sea**
The Rutford Ice Stream moves about 3 ft 3 in (1 m) each day.

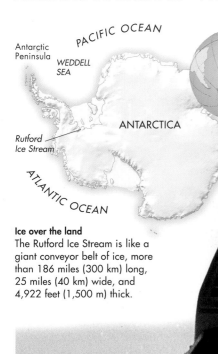

Clothes and boots are kept dry for warmth.

Gloves are always worn – bare hands against cold metal can cause frostbite.

Food is stored on the back of the snowmobile.

Chisel and pole for probing crevasses

ski-doo

# Clean air...
# Dirty air

**T**here is nothing new about dirty air. In the past, when most homes had coal or wood heating, city air was so sooty that it turned buildings black. Today, fewer people have fires at home, but we have other sources of air pollution instead. They include products that release airborne chemicals when they are used, and household garbage that gives off toxic substances when it is burned. But the most significant sources of dirty air are fossil fuels, which include coal, oil, and natural gas. They are burned by power stations, and by cars, trucks, buses, and planes.

> 66 I live in Los Angeles, California, and there is a lot of smog here sometimes. Smog is a type of pollution that you can't get away from. It's full of chemicals and dust, junk, and yucky stuff. When it gets in your lungs you can only breathe for about a second, and you feel like you're going to keep coughing for the rest of your life. When you run, it's even harder because then you really feel like you can't breathe at all. Since I have asthma, my lungs are a bit more sensitive, so I really feel the difference when there's a smog alert. 99
>
> *Sophia Leikin*

## City smog

Bangkok, Thailand, is covered in a yellow smog on a sunny day. This is a serious problem in cities with a warm climate. Smog is produced when gases from car exhausts react with sunlight. The result is a choking brown haze that contains nitrogen oxides, ozone, and other poisonous gases. Many cities have smog alerts when conditions are very bad.

**Fuel from sugarcane**
The sap is extracted from sugarcane and fermented to turn the sugar into ethanol.

## Low-pollution fuel

To tackle the smog problem, scientists have tried out fuels that create less pollution. Ethanol is one alternative. It is made from plants such as sugarcane, and it burns cleanly, producing carbon dioxide and water. But ethanol is more expensive than gasoline.

**Clean run**
This Swedish bus is powered by ethanol, which can be burned on its own, or can be mixed with petrol.

## Acid rain

When coal or oil are burned, they release sulfur dioxide, a highly acidic gas. Once this gas is in the atmosphere, it dissolves in droplets of moisture and produces acid rain, which makes trees sicken and die. Acid rain also harms wildlife in lakes and rivers, and eats into stone buildings. Modern power stations have cleaning systems that remove sulfur dioxide from their smoke, but cars do not.

**Acid attack**
This ancient statue has lost its head and arms. The culprit is acid rain, which has slowly weakened the stone.

**Dying trees**
Acid rain has changed the chemistry of the soil and damaged these spruce trees. They are suffering from dieback, which is when the young shoots die.

### ACID RAIN

*EXPERIMENT*

**You will need:** 2 pieces of blackboard chalk, 2 jars, some vinegar, and tap water.

**1 POUR WATER** into one jar until it is a third full. Pour vinegar into the other jar until it is also a third full. Drop one piece of chalk into each jar. Leave overnight.

**2 LOOK AT THE JARS** the next day. The chalk in the vinegar has been eaten away and partially dissolved. The chalk in the water is still whole.

**This shows that:** although it is a weak acid, vinegar can dissolve chalk. Acid rain eats into chalk and limestone in just the same way.

In cold places, **winter air** pollution produces **acid snow** that can taste as **sour** as a **lemon**

The **damage** to the **ozone layer** caused by **CFCs** will not be fully repaired until **2050** at the earliest

## Ozone rescue

At ground level, ozone gas is dangerous. But high up above the ground, it forms a natural shield that protects us from the Sun's ultraviolet light. In recent years, this layer has been eaten away by CFCs, which are chemicals once used in aerosols, fridges, and plastic packaging. In 1987, an international agreement came into force to phase out CFCs.

Today's aerosols are CFC-free.

**Aerosol can**
CFCs, sprayed from aerosol cans like this one, take more than 100 years to go away.

CFCs can leak from fridges that are thrown away.

# PRECIOUS

**W**ater is essential for life. In some parts of the world, fresh water is easy for people and animals to find, but in others it is hidden underground. But wherever it is, water moves in a continuous cycle. It falls to Earth as rain or snow and makes its way to the oceans, either above or below ground. Every day the Sun's heat evaporates billions of tons of water from the oceans. Water vapor forms clouds and falls again as fresh rainwater. At one time, humans made little impact on this cycle, but in the past 100 years, this has changed. We now use so much fresh water in our homes and industry that, in some places, supplies are running out.

"Human demands are about to collide with the ability of the hydrological cycle to supply water."

FOOD AND AGRICULTURE ORGANIZATION

## Surface water

Tumbling down a rocky hillside in Oregon, water races toward its meeting with the sea. This is surface water – water that is found above the ground. Surface water includes ice caps, rivers, and lakes. Water is vital to all living things because they need it for essential processes such as feeding and breathing.

# RESOURCE

Long beak can reach insects, snails, and small frogs.

Brown plumage helps the bird camouflage itself among the reeds.

Long widely splayed toes prevent the bird from sinking into soft ground.

## Drying out

Many birds, such as this water rail, live in freshwater wetlands and depend on them to survive. Sometimes the water is diverted or drained away to make new land for houses or farms. When this happens, wetland birds are forced out. Because they cannot adapt to other habitats, they often die.

## Underground water

In some desert regions, the only place you can find water is below the ground. These women are drawing water from a well in Mali, on the edge of the Sahara desert. The water first falls as rain. It trickles through the rocks and collects in natural reservoirs deep under the ground.

| United States | Australia | United Kingdom | Kenya |
|---|---|---|---|
| 411,400 gallons (1,870,000 liters) | 332,200 gallons (1,510,000 liters) | 45,100 gallons (205,000 liters) | 18,920 gallons (86,000 liters) |

## One year's water

Some countries use far more water than others. The amount of water one person uses in a year is shown by these buckets. The figures include water used for drinking and washing, as well as in industry and farming. Huge amounts are sprayed onto crops. Making just one car uses 8,000 gallons (30,000 liters) of water.

## ACTION!
### SAVE WATER

Put a brick in your lavatory cistern – when you flush, less water is used.

Take a shower instead of a bath.

Use a bowl of water for washing instead of a running tap.

---

## NATURAL WATER FILTER

*EXPERIMENT*

**You will need:** scissors, plastic bottle, pair of compasses, large plate, pair of protective gloves, spoon, pebbles, gravel, small stones, coarse sand, fine sand, jug, water, soil.

**1 USING THE** scissors, cut the top off the bottle. With the compasses, carefully pierce about six small holes around the side of the bottle, near the base.

Pierce holes with point of compasses

**2 STAND THE BOTTLE** on the plate. Put on the gloves. Spoon in the pebbles, then the gravel, followed by the small stones. Spoon in the coarse sand and then the fine sand.

Soil collects as water is filtered

**3 PUT A HANDFUL** of soil into a jug half-full of water. Stir it thoroughly, and then pour the mixture into the open top of the bottle. The water that collects on the plate will be much cleaner than the water in the jug.

Small stones

Coarse sand

Fine sand

### This shows that:
water is naturally filtered as it flows through the ground.

Some 3 million people are made homeless by floods every year, many of them in coastal zones

# FLOOD!

I**magine being** swamped by waist-high water, while everything you own is washed away. This happens somewhere in the world almost every week. Floods also destroy crops and increase the risk of disease. Flooding is a natural occurrence and can be useful. For example, in tropical countries such as Bangladesh, monsoon floods spread silt that fertilizes fields. But most floods are harmful, and their effects are getting worse. One reason for this is that more people now live in areas prone to floods. Another is that the world's climate is changing, making floods more severe.

### Sinking feeling

Floods are not always caused by rain. In the region around Venice, in northern Italy, floods have worsened because a lot of fresh water has been pumped out of the ground. This has made the ground sink, carrying the city with it. At high tide, the sea now floods many of Venice's famous squares, and tourists have to use wooden walkways.

### Monsoon flooding

Countries near the Equator have wet and dry seasons instead of hot and cold ones. In southern Asia, the wet season, or monsoon, starts with violent thunderstorms that can drop more than 12 in (30 cm) of rain in a day. These downpours make it difficult to get around, particularly in low-lying places where the water drains slowly.

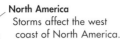

**North America**
Storms affect the west coast of North America.

**South America**
During an El Niño year, the sea off South America gets warmer.

**El Niño rain**
Ecuador and Peru receive more rain than normal.

High tides threaten low-lying cities in northern Europe.

NORTH AMERICA

EUROPE

ASIA

ATLANTIC OCEAN

River flooding affects areas of southeastern US.

PACIFIC OCEAN

AFRICA

Monsoons cause flooding around the Bay of Bengal.

INDIAN OCEAN

The Amazon River bursts its banks during its annual flood.

SOUTH AMERICA

Wet-season floods can affect parts of central Africa.

Tropical storms can cause flooding in Northern Australia.

AUSTRALASIA

El Niño causes storm floods on the Pacific coast of South America.

**Annual Rainfall**

More than 78 in (2,000 mm)

20–78 in (500–2,000 mm)

Less than 20 in (500 mm)

## El Niño

The west coast of South America is normally one of the driest places on Earth, but every three or four years the weather pattern changes. The sea warms up, fish disappear, and freak storms cause mudslides that can wash houses away. This weather disturbance, called El Niño, is part of a natural cycle.

## Flood risk areas

Your chances of being hit by a flood depend on where you live. This world map shows annual rainfall. In the tropics, monsoon rain and tropical storms cause floods. In other parts of the world, heavy rain makes rivers burst their banks and floods occur. Earthquakes can also produce flooding because they trigger tidal waves.

Between 1986 and 1995, **floods** were responsible for more than **half** of all **fatalities** caused by natural catastrophes

## Global warming
causes **more storms** and heavier **rains**, and increases **flooding**

"I live in Assam, India, where it rains a lot. When the rivers start to rise, school closes, which is fun at first, but then it gets boring. The bazaars close too, so my mother has to stock up on rice and vegetables. Once during the floods, a whole lot of dirty brown water flowed into the house. My mother, sister, and I ran upstairs to the roof and huddled under two black umbrellas, while my father and grandfather picked up whatever boxes and dishes they could save and brought them up. I was quite scared."

*Pinaki Roy*

## Burst banks

Working against the clock, these people are building an artificial bank to hold back the Missouri River. Permanent artificial banks can prevent floods in normal years, but they can make flood water pile up after very heavy rain. If a bank breaks, this pent-up water suddenly pours onto the land, with disastrous results.

**HYDROLOGIST**
JONATHAN DENISON

JONATHAN DENISON'S JOB IS TO HELP PEOPLE PLAN HOW BEST TO USE WATER FROM LOCAL rivers. He works in East Africa where rivers often flood during the rainy season but dry up in the dry season. Jonathan advises on dams that can store floodwater in the rainy season for use when the rivers are dry.

**Aerial view of the wilderness area**
The Zambezi Valley is a vast plain with meandering rivers and forested areas that are rich in wildlife.

## A day in the life of a HYDROLOGIST

It is important to design dams and weirs so that they have the least environmental impact and still provide enough water for local needs.

**Taking readings**
Team members use special equipment to measure the river water levels in the wilderness area.

**Today, Jonathan** and his colleagues investigate two possible intake sites for a pipeline to take water from a tributary of the Zambezi River to an irrigation program in the Zambezi Valley.

**6:00am** I get up early, having checked and packed all the equipment the night before. Vital to the trip is the GPS (Global Positioning System) backpack that will be used to establish the position and height of the river at the intakes. It will receive information from four or more satellites as well as a ground-based station, and give us a reading in three directions (sideways, forward, and up/down).

**6:45am** I meet up with the surveyor, engineer, and environmentalist. We will pick up the game ranger later. The valley is a sustainable hunting reserve where hunters pay to shoot crocodiles, buffalo, and elephants. Part of their fees goes to the local communities. Some people disagree with this, others say it is the only way to preserve the herds of animals. Everyone agrees our engineering designs must have a minimal impact on the wilderness.

**7:00am** The helicopter lifts off. It's midsummer and we are dressed for the heat (bush pants, long shirts, hats) and carrying lots of water. We plan to walk along the proposed pipeline route to see if it can be built with minimal impact to the forested environment. Our other option is to build a tunnel through the mountainside.

**Equipment**
Binoculars are used to find the way in the thick bush.

**Binoculars**

**8:00am** We collect the armed game ranger and fly low across the tree tops and drop down into the winding gorge. Using aerial photographs we guide the pilot to the site, where he lands with some difficulty. We walk to the first intake site – sometimes following "tunnels" made by elephants in the high grass. The temperature is already hot and we are dripping with sweat. We check our position with the GPS and photographs, and confirm that we are at the correct bend in the river.

**River dwellers**
The habitat of crocodiles and fish must not be harmed by the construction work.

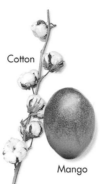

Cotton

Mango

**Crops**
Farmers may grow crops of cotton or fruit, such as mango.

> **You need to respond to people and their environment but keep technically realistic.**

GPS receiver    GPS carrier

**Accurate locations**
The portable Global Positioning System provides accurate details about location, using satellite signals.

**Water supplies**
Irrigation helps people grow more food for sale to markets to make a living.

**10:00am** First, we inspect the riverbed and banks and decide on the best position for the weir. The surveyor carries the GPS backpack and a small satellite dish on an aluminum pole. He records the coordinates of the points we decide on with a hand-held computer. These points will allow us to draw a cross-section of the river at six places up and downstream of the weir site. This helps us calculate flood levels. I photograph the area for additional reference.

**Floodwater!**
Hydrologists estimate the size of floods so engineers can design bridges and dams to pass the floods safely.

**10:30am** We return to the helicopter along the possible pipeline route. At one bend we discover the bank is vertical, so the pipe would have to take another route. We follow a route away from the river, taking readings as we go. All of us agree that the pipeline is possible, but would scar the environment during construction. The impact could be reduced by painting the pipe green, but the path cut through the bush would still be easy to see. A greater concern is the need for a road alongside the pipe for future repairs. This would allow people to drive into the wilderness area, and could make poaching and illegal deforestation a problem.

**12:00pm** Time for lunch before we walk out of the gorge. Two of the team are exhausted and return to camp by helicopter. The surveyor, game ranger, and I head for the site where the tunnel will enter the mountain. We survey this site and record data. I take photos of the tunnel entrance and sketch the surrounding area. Although the tunnel would disturb the environment less (it could be excavated from the other side), it may well cost more than the pipeline. However, only limited building work would be needed and the bush would grow back.

**3:00pm** Finally, we return to the first site and continue surveying. We must collect enough data to prepare a design of both options. Only then can we decide which solution is the best, in terms of cost, building time, and impact on the environment.

**7:00pm** It's dark when we meet the four-wheel drive vehicle for the return. Tomorrow we'll download the data and produce the drawings. It will take about two months of engineering work before we know which option will be best. Judging from today's work, the tunnel seems the best way to preserve the wilderness area.

**Map of southeastern Africa**
The Zambezi River flows from Zambia through Mozambique and then empties into the Indian Ocean.

The bridge allows people to cross the river downstream.

# Water Pollution

**O**nce water is used, it does not simply disappear. Sooner or later it finds its way back into nature's water cycle, which eventually takes it to the sea. But used water is often polluted with waste from factories, farms, and homes. Some of this waste can harm animals and plants that live in water, while other waste causes disease. In the world's richest countries, water pollution has been a problem for a long time, although now tighter regulations are reducing the damage. But in many poorer countries, pollution is increasing, and clean water can be hard to find.

### Chemical waste
One look at this stream shows that its water is unsafe to drink, or even to touch. But polluted water is not always this easy to spot. Some waste chemicals dissolve without leaving any visible traces, which makes them difficult to control.

Gas from this cylinder is burned to speed up the process of extracting gold.

Miner wears no protective gloves and can get skin poisoning from the mercury.

### Mercury in the Amazon
This Brazilian miner is extracting gold by mixing it with mercury. Once the gold has been purified, the mercury is often dumped in rivers. Mercury kills freshwater wildlife, and can poison people if it gets into drinking water.

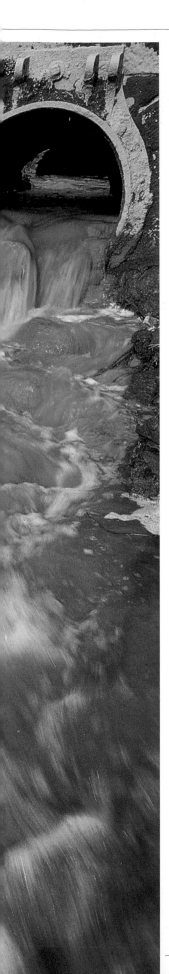

Some rivers in the world are so polluted with industrial and agricultural waste that they are said to be biologically dead.

### Oil on shore

Volunteers are cleaning up oil that has been washed onto a beach in Wales. Oil spills like this can be deadly to sea birds. The oil clogs up feathers, making it impossible for the bird to fly and hard for it to stay warm.

A bird may swallow oil when preening its feathers.

Oil can be removed with washing-up liquid.

### In hot water

Oil refineries and power stations often use cold water to get rid of unwanted heat. The water, which becomes hot, is poured into rivers like this one. Heat reduces the amount of oxygen that the river water can hold, which can cause fish to die.

### ACTION!
### STOP POLLUTION

If you see signs of pollution, such as oil, on beaches, inform local officials.

Do not drop litter into rivers, into the sea, or onto beaches.

Take unused paint to your local recycling center.

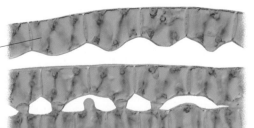

Each algal strand is thinner than a hair.

When millions of these strands cover the water, the result is called "algal bloom."

### Going for growth

Microscopic algae like these grow in rivers, lakes, and ponds, and normally cause no harm. But if fertilizer or sewage pollutes the water, they grow much faster. The algae use up oxygen when they die and rot away, leaving little for the other water wildlife.

# OUR LAND
## OUR FUTURE

PEOPLE FIRST STARTED TO FARM MORE THAN 10,000 YEARS AGO. THEY BEGAN A WAVE OF LAND CLEARANCE THAT changed the face of the Earth. Today, we need land more than ever – to grow crops to feed our growing population and to build homes. The way we use land has far-reaching effects on all forms of life.

In spring, a vast carpet of bluebonnets covers the rolling plains of western Texas (main picture). This open prairie is a natural landscape and home to many plant and animal species. Thousands of miles further south, a tropical rain forest has been devastated (inset). The trees were cleared to farm cattle.

“ The sky is held up by the trees. If the forest disappears, the sky-roof of the world collapses. Nature and man then perish together. ”

**ANCIENT SAYING OF THE NATIVE AMERICANS**

# *Soil* EROSION

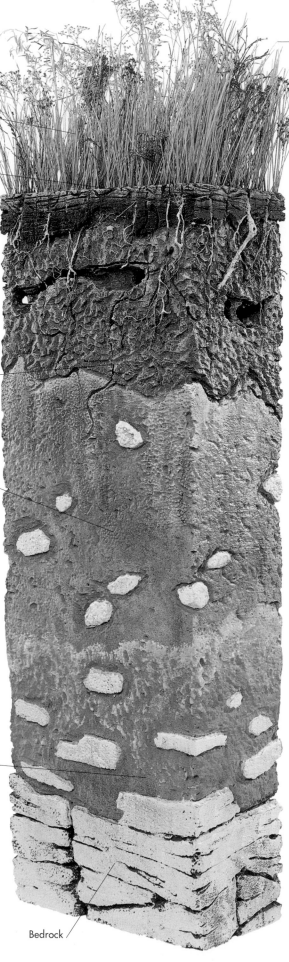

**Plants**
Roots carry moisture held in the topsoil to plants above the ground.

**Ground level**
Some humus is found on the ground's surface where dead plant matter has decomposed.

**Topsoil**
The first layer of soil is called topsoil. It is held together by plant roots and contains humus.

**Subsoil**
This contains less humus than topsoil.

**Bedrock particles**
Moisture and soil chemicals slowly break the bedrock into fragments.

Bedrock

Few of us think about the soil beneath our feet. However, plants grow in soil and all land creatures rely, directly or indirectly, on plants for food. In nature, soil is made all the time, but it is also eroded, or worn away. Both these processes happen very slowly, and they are usually balanced so that the amount of soil stays the same. But when land is plowed up or overgrazed, this balance can quickly change. Erosion can speed up by over a thousand times, so that soil starts to disappear. Fortunately, erosion can be brought under control. With so many people to feed, soil is much too precious to lose.

## How soil is made

Soil develops from a layer of loose, weathered rock fragments. Chemicals released by animal or plant remains, known as humus, transform the rock fragments into soil. The soil forms layers. The top layer, called topsoil, is the most fertile.

## Dust storms

These women in Tunisia are walking through a dust storm. In dry places like this, there is little plant cover and the soil is easily blown away. In wet places, plant roots hold the soil in place, but if the plants are cleared for farming, the soil can be swept away by wind.

# From 1945 to 2000, more than one-sixth of the world's productive land was spoiled by soil erosion.

## Gulley erosion

Grazing cattle have stripped away the plant cover on these Canadian hillsides. Rain has then washed off the topsoil, gouging out deep gulleys. Once erosion gets this bad, it is very difficult for plants to grow back.

**Nature** can take more than a **century** to **make** just **1 in** (2.5 cm) of **soil**

## Farming in terraces

In southeast Asia, terraces are often used to prevent soil erosion. They hold back the soil when it rains, making sure that it does not wash away. In other parts of the world, farmers sometimes make mini-terraces by plowing along slopes, instead of up and down.

## Flood damage

After a heavy storm, this section of road in California has been washed away. Eroded hillsides increase this kind of damage because rain rushes off them, sweeping away anything in its path. Where the soil is still in place, it soaks up water like a sponge, making flood damage less severe.

On average, each **acre** of **farmland** in America loses **17 tons** of **soil** a year

---

## SOIL EROSION

**EXPERIMENT**

**You will need:** potted plant, pot filled with soil, 2 plastic cups, watering can.

**3** **WATCH THE WATER** as it flows through the pots. It passes quickly through the pot without the plant, carrying soil with it. In the pot with the plant, it flows more slowly and is clearer.

**1** **FIT THE POTTED PLANT** into the neck of one of the plastic cups. Fit the pot containing only soil into the neck of the other cup.

**2** **USING THE WATERING CAN,** gently pour the same amount of water into both pots.

**This shows that:** plant roots hold soil together and protect it from erosion.

# FARM ALARM

## Airborne attack

Skimming over a field in California, a plane sprays pesticides on the crop below. Pesticides help farmers to produce big harvests, but they have harmful side effects. They often kill useful animals as well as pests, and they also end up in our food.

Colorado beetle grubs

## Pest alert

Colorado beetle grubs eat potato and tomato leaves. For pests like these, big fields provide an almost endless supply of food.

W ith more people than ever on Earth, we need all the food we can grow. During the last 40 years, scientists have developed many ways to boost harvests so that we get more from the land that is farmed. Heavy machinery makes light work of jobs that once took weeks, while fertilizers and pesticides help to produce record yields. Special breeding programs have improved the crops, and genetic engineering may improve them even more. However, this kind of farming has drawbacks. Unlike traditional farming techniques, it affects wildlife and may also reduce the natural fertility of the soil. Used wisely, the land can support both farming and wildlife.

Harvest mouse nibbling on a plant stem

## Battery hens

These chickens will spend their lives in small cages that allow thousands of them to be raised side by side. Intensive farming of this kind makes eggs cheap, but the chickens suffer because they have no room to move.

## Lost wildlife

Many wild animals, such as this harvest mouse, are harmed by modern farming methods. In Europe, harvest mice were once common in cereal fields. Today, their nests are often destroyed by combine harvesters, making it hard for them to survive.

## Natural help

On organic farms, like this one in England, artificial pesticides are never used. Instead, pests are controlled by swapping the crops around each year, and by using some plants to lure pests away from others. Here, rows of potato plants are growing next to mustard, which has bright yellow flowers. The mustard plants act only as a decoy to attract flying insects away from the potatoes.

Organic farming works **with nature** rather than **against it**

## Asian organics

Organic farming is not a new idea – in some places it has been used for thousands of years. On traditional Chinese farms, manure from farm animals is used to keep the soil fertile. Additionally, waste food is used to raise pigs, poultry, and fish.

A combine harvester works fast and can reap the crop while the grain is at its best.

The wheat is emptied into a tractor-drawn trailer.

Each **year** the world's **farmers** use more than **110 million** tons of artificial fertilizer

Traces of pesticide can be **found** in almost all of **the nonorganic food** that we eat

## Large-scale farming

These wheat fields in the US produce huge harvests that help to feed people around the world. But this kind of intensive farming causes problems for the environment. It relies heavily on pesticides and other agricultural chemicals that damage the soil. It also uses fossil fuels to drive farm machinery.

# ACTION!
## BE AWARE

Help cut down on pesticide use by eating organic food.

Avoid food that comes from animals raised indoors.

Try growing your own vegetables – in a pot or in the garden.

## Genetically modified crops

Although they look like ordinary plants, these soybeans have been given extra genes that make them easier to grow. Many scientists believe that such genetically modified (GM) crops will help farmers grow more food without harming the environment. Others are concerned that they may cause problems by passing on the new genes to plants in the wild.

**ORGANIC FARMER**
LARRAINE YEAGER

LARRAINE YEAGER'S LIFE ON HER FARM IN INDIANA IS BOTH HARD WORK AND FUN. EACH SEASON BRINGS NEW CHALLENGES AND REWARDS FOR HER AND her husband. They keep chickens, goats, sheep, pigs, and cows. Tomatoes, corn, and other crops are grown using organic methods that promote healthy soil and plants.

**The working day**
A regular check is made on Babe, as she is due to give birth very soon.

# A day in the life of an
# ORGANIC FARMER

## Organic farming is a sustainable system that maintains the long-term fertility of the soil and uses less of Earth's resources.

Corn

Hay

**Animal feed**
All the animal feed on the farm is organic.

Chaff and molasses

**Today, Larraine** and her husband wake up early for a busy summer's day on Wellspring Farm.

**6:30am** Time to feed and water the animals. The animals live in the barn with separate areas for pasture and grazing. The chickens have a special house called a coop.

**Chicken house**
Free-range chickens need a coop where they can lay and sit on their eggs.

Chick and corn

It has nest boxes in it where the chickens lay their eggs. We feed the sheep and goats with corn and hay, then turn them out into the fields where they nibble pasture during the day. Willow, our Morgan horse, loves his feed because it has molasses in it which helps to keep him healthy. When we take the feed to our sow we see she is getting ready to farrow (give birth to baby pigs). She is kept in a special enclosed pen called a farrowing pen, ready for the forthcoming birth of her piglets.

**8:00am** With the feeding done, it's time to look after the plants. Those in the greenhouse need extra water on warm days, so I water them now as well as later in the afternoon. Plants grow quickly in this greenhouse because of the year-round warmth and sunlight. At the moment we have lettuce, green peppers, flowers, and herb plants in the seedling flats.

**Lettuce seedlings**
These will later be transplanted into the garden.

Green pepper

**9:00am** Our two new Holstein calves have to be bottle-fed every few hours. They suck eagerly on their bottles of warm milk. Soon, they will be able to drink directly from a bucket. Already they are starting to munch on some hay, and we cannot resist taking a few minutes just to pet them.

**10:30am** Now it is time to visit the chicken coop to gather eggs. Each hen lays one egg a day, although sometimes they skip a day. I notice that one of the hens has chosen to sit on her eggs. I do not bother her – chickens are very protective while they are sitting on eggs.

**Collecting hay**
Hay, grass that is cut and dried, is stored and used as animal feed (fodder).

> "Buying organic food helps support farmers who have adopted environmentally friendly methods of production."

**11:00am** The vegetable garden is lush with summer growth, but so are the weeds! I use several different techniques to get rid of them. The rototiller is a mechanical tool that weeds between the garden rows by tilling the ground. I hand weed close to the plants to avoid damaging them. We also put a thick layer of mulch (old vegetable matter) around the plants and in the rows. This helps to prevent weed growth and holds moisture in the soil.

**12:20pm** During my lunch break, I glance through the new seed catalog that came in the mail. There are some irresistible new varieties of vegetables listed that should be fun to try next spring.

**1:30pm** We drive over to the wheat field to see if it is ready for harvesting. It is bright and golden, but the wheat tops, or heads, are not yet bent over. It will be about another week before the wheat is ready to harvest. We grind our own wheat through the year and use it to make delicious wholewheat bread.

**2:30pm** There are some areas of the garden that have already been harvested so I want to replant them today. We have a small wagon-load full of manure from cleaning out the barn, which we have mixed with old hay used for animal bedding. I use a pitchfork to spread the manure and hay evenly on the garden area I have just tilled. Then I retill the area until the soil is smooth. I will probably plant green beans in this spot, and set out some lettuce plants from the greenhouse. The chickens come over while I am working – they love to explore freshly tilled ground.

**5:00pm** We have one hive of bees near the garden so that they can help to pollinate the garden plants. About 33,000 bees live in this one hive. The bees work more effectively if we feed them with sugar water once a week. So, after putting on my beekeeper suit, veiled hat, and long-sleeved gloves, I open the top of the hive and pour sugar water into a special box inside the hive. The bees are busy

**Tending the beehives**
Sometimes the bees need to be subdued with a smoker.

Protective mask

Hive

Smoker

inside the hive, but if they start to behave aggressivly. I have a tool called a smoker that can subdue them temporarily.

**7:30pm** With the feeding chores done, I check on Babe. She is starting to farrow, which is exciting news for our family. During the next hour and a half she gives birth to piglets! We towel each one dry when it's born and put it under a heat lamp. It's late by the time we finish, but the rewards of organic farming are worth the effort.

**Wellspring Farm**
Larraine's farm lies in the state of Indiana, which has very cold winters but generally hot summer days.

Each piglet weighs about 5 lb (2.3 kg)

**Feeding the piglets**
Soon after the piglets are born, they start to drink milk (suckle) from their mother.

# HABITATS *at risk*

**M**ost living things rely on a particular type of habitat. For example, giant clams are found only in coral reefs, while the world's largest trees – giant sequoias – grow on mountain slopes. Habitats are much more than places to live, because they provide everything that different plants or animals need to survive. However, all over the world, habitats are under threat. Some are being destroyed by farming, by logging, or by building, while others are being altered by drainage, pollution, or climate change. Our efforts to conserve natural habitats and their wildlife are more important than ever before.

" I live in England. I sponsor an elephant called Malaika through a charity called Care For The Wild. Malaika is eight years old and lives in Kenya. She was rescued because she was on land that the villagers lived on. The elephants were there first but the villagers had used the land to grow crops and build homes. When the elephants were on the land, the villagers would kill them. Malaika's parents were killed when she was a baby. Malaika was taken to the Care For The Wild orphanage. "

*J Quigly*

## Tourism

Wherever people travel, habitats may become damaged. These tourists are in Antarctica – one of the most remote places on Earth. Antarctica is the cleanest continent, but with more visitors every year, this could change.

## Arctic and Antarctica

The polar regions are the last true wildernesses left on Earth, but even here habitat change has taken place. Pipelines now carry oil and gas across the Arctic tundra. Increasing numbers of passenger ships visit Antarctica's shores. More importantly, global warming is melting the polar ice, disrupting the lives of many animals, including penguins.

Adélie penguins need unpolluted seas to survive.

## Conservation

Resting in the heat, these rare Asiatic lions live in a protected habitat – the forest in India's Gir National Park. The lions depend on the forest, but it is under threat from farmers who are desperate for land. Shortage of land makes conservation difficult in many parts of the world. Growing enough food for people means less room for wildlife.

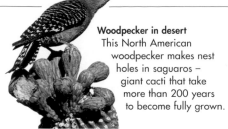

**Woodpecker in desert**
This North American woodpecker makes nest holes in saguaros – giant cacti that take more than 200 years to become fully grown.

# Desert life

Plants in the Sonoran desert (right) can cope with droughts, but they grow much more slowly than plants in most other habitats. If they are damaged – by cars or motorcycles being driven off-road – it can take years for them to recover. Desert animals need plants to survive, so any damage harms them as well.

**Tortoise in desert**
The rare desert tortoise lives in the southwest US and northern Mexico. It eats desert plants and its shell protects it from the extreme heat.

# Wetlands

This marina in Florida was once a coastal wetland – a natural habitat for alligators and wading birds. After forests, wetlands are among the most threatened habitats in the world. Some have been completely destroyed, but others are now protected by an international agreement aimed at conserving wetland life.

# Coral reef

In this reef off the Bahamas, a plastic bag has caught on some elkhorn coral. Pollution is one of the reasons that the world's coral reefs are in trouble. Reefs are also damaged by dredging and by fishing. Rising sea temperatures – a result of global warming – affect the reefs' algae and disturb the balanced ecosystem.

## ACTION!
### SAVE IT

Do not buy coral or shells – they may have been collected live from a reef.

Never throw trash into the sea.

Do not walk across restricted land in conservation areas.

# Grasslands

At one time, natural grassland covered the whole of the American Midwest, and large parts of other continents. However, in the last 100 years, most of the grassland has been plowed up. For grassland animals, such as the prairie dog, there is less space for survival.

The prairie dog's home is in a burrow underground.

# Forest Crisis

## Temperate rain forest

These moss-covered trees form part of a unique habitat, the temperate rain forest of the American northwest. Temperate rain forests are found in areas of high rainfall and cool temperatures. These forests once covered a vast area and contained giant coniferous trees many centuries old. Today, most of the original forest has been replaced by planted forest with much less wildlife.

**About** one-third of the **Earth's** original **forests** have been **cut down**

## Tropical rain forest

The Amazon River winds through tropical rain forest in Brazil. Tropical rain forests are found in the hot, wet climate zone near the Equator. They contain a huge variety of trees, such as mahogany and rosewood, and many other plants – some that scientists have yet to identify. Each tree provides food for many animals, from orangutans to tiny insects.

**F**orests contain more living creatures and plants than any other habitat on land. They are home to more than 10,000 different types of trees, and at least half a million types of animals. But this wealth of life is under threat because the world's forests are being cut down to provide timber, and to make way for farms, buildings, and roads. In some parts of the world, including Europe and Asia, deforestation started long ago. But in the tropics, where forest wildlife is richest, large-scale deforestation has been underway for less than 40 years. Today, tropical rain forests are disappearing at a record rate.

## Disappearing trees

This land in Borneo has been stripped of its trees and is criss-crossed by tracks and newly dug terraces. The timber from tropical rain forests is often very good at resisting decay, and is used to make outdoor furniture. Every time people buy products made from this wood, more forest is cleared to keep up the supply.

## ACTION!
### SAVE WOOD

Do not buy products made of tropical hardwood unless the wood has been grown in a sustainable way.

Recycle paper – it saves cutting down more trees.

" Forests do wonderful things. They bind soil to the ground, regulate water supplies, and help govern the climate. "

UNITED NATIONS DEVELOPMENT PROGRAM: HUMAN DEVELOPMENT REPORT 1998

## Plants at risk

In tropical rain forests, many plants live high up in trees – their roots clinging to branches. Called epiphytes, they collect moisture from rain and nutrients from dead leaves and dust. When forests are cleared, epiphytes die since they cannot survive on the ground.

Epiphytic orchid from forest in the Himalayas

## Sustainable wood

This worker is using sustainable wood to make top-quality guitars. Sustainable wood is usually grown on plantations. Young trees are planted when old ones are cut down, so the supply never runs out. The rich ecosystems of rain forests – the traditional source of wood for musical instruments – can remain untouched.

## People at risk

When forests are cut down, people can be harmed just as much as wildlife. This woman belongs to the Kayan tribe from the Burma-Thailand border – an area where the forest is under threat from logging. Like other people in the tropics, the Kayan rely on the forest for their livelihood. Without it, their traditional way of life ends.

**Brazil** has formulated **laws** and **regulations** to **reverse** deforestation

# FIRE

For millions of years, fires have been a natural feature of the living world. They burn off dead wood and leaves, clearing the ground for new plants to grow. But when people start fires – either deliberately or by accident – this natural balance is often upset. Accidental blazes, sparked off by campfires or cigarettes, can be very destructive because they may quickly get out of control. They happen more often than natural fires, so trees have less time to recover. But for wildlife, the worst fires are deliberate ones designed to clear away forest. After these fires, the ground is converted into fields, leaving forest plants and animals without a home.

## Forest fire

As flames sweep through a forest, they can destroy trees that may have taken more than 200 years to grow. Birds and large mammals can usually escape the flames, but most small animals are burned alive as the inferno overtakes them. After a major blaze, new saplings soon sprout, but it can take decades for the forest's wildlife to fully recover.

## Animals at risk

Southeast Asia's forest fires are very dangerous for endangered orangutans. These apes climb to higher branches, but this cannot save them from the flames. Lemurs living in Madagascar's rain forest, also have no way to escape from fire.

## Out of the ashes

Fire does not always kill trees because some have defenses against the flames. In fact, certain kinds of pine trees depend on fire, and will not drop their seeds until their cones have been scorched. Forest-floor plants burn away above ground, but their roots remain safe.

Bulbs are protected under the ground.

**Safety underground**
Trout lilies can survive fires because they grow from bulbs which are protected from the flames.

**Fireproof bark**
Many eucalyptus trees have peeling bark. If the bark catches fire, it falls away without damaging the tree.

# ALERT

"Fires ... are one of the greatest ecological disasters of the millennium."

KLAUS TOPFER
HEAD OF UNITED NATIONS
ENVIRONMENT PROGRAM (UNEP)

## ACTION!
### PREVENT FIRES

Do not leave empty bottles on the ground – they can focus the Sun's rays, triggering a fire.

Never play with fire – a single dropped match can start a blaze.

If you spot a fire, call the local fire department immediately.

**Feeding**
The stork's long beak is not harmed if it touches the hot remains of the fire.

**Putting out the flames**
Hovering above the flames, a helicopter uses a "bambi bucket" to drop water on a bush fire. The bucket is refilled by dipping it in a nearby lake.

"My name is Sophie Vearing and I live just outside the city of Wagga Wagga in New South Wales, Australia. We have very hot days in the summer and the landscape turns from green to golden brown. The temperature can reach 111°F (44°C), and because there is a very high danger of bush fires, you are not allowed to light fires at all. My stepfather, who is a Group Captain in the Rural Fire Service, is ready to be called to a fire at any time."

*Sophie Vearing*

## Animal gains

Attracted by the sight of smoke, this African marabou stork has caught an animal trying to escape from a grassland fire. When a fire burns out, marabous often search the burned grass for the roasted bodies of grasshoppers and lizards.

## Grassland fires

Dry grass catches fire very easily, which is why grasslands, such as these in India, burn more often than forests. Grass fires do not produce much heat, and the grass soon grows again from its roots, because they are kept safe below the ground.

**Blue whale**
North Atlantic, North Pacific,
and southern hemisphere
Estimated numbers left: 10,000
Hunted by the whaling industry

**Green turtle**
Warm tropical oceans
Estimated numbers left: 600,000
Turtles have a low reproductive rate
Hunted for food, shells, and eggs

**St. Helena earwig**
St. Helena, South Atlantic
Estimated numbers left: unknown
The decline may be due to introduction
of other animals into the environment

**Black rhinoceros**
Central and southern Africa
Estimated numbers left: 2,000
Hunted for their horns for medicine
Habitat taken over by agriculture

# Animals IN DANGER

Up to **a dozen** species of **insect** become **extinct** every **day**

## All over the world, wild animals are faced with an increasing struggle to survive. Deciding which species are

most threatened, and how we can help them, is one of the most important tasks facing biologists today. Many endangered species are protected by laws against hunting and by international agreements that stop them from being sold. In extreme cases, some have even been brought back from the brink of extinction by breeding them in captivity and releasing their young back into the wild. But for most wild animals, the best safeguard is an unspoiled natural habitat. If they have this, they can look after themselves.

### Clones without homes

The giant panda is probably the world's most famous endangered animal. It lives in the bamboo forests of China, a habitat that is steadily shrinking as the land is taken over for farming and building houses. Some scientists think that pandas can be saved by cloning, which would increase their numbers by producing young animals from a mother's cells. But without the bamboo forest, cloned pandas could not survive in the wild.

## In the red

Endangered species are monitored by the International Union for the Conservation of Nature (IUCN). This organization publishes "Red Lists" of endangered animals and plants, showing how much danger they are in. These five animals (left) are on the "critically endangered" list – the highest category of threat. Without help, they could soon become extinct.

**Rothschild Mynah**
Bali, Indonesia
Estimated numbers left: 800
Illegal capture for
cage-bird trade

## Big and beautiful

Big cats are beautiful and glamorous, which means that when they are threatened, they make the headlines and attract funds for their protection. Although it is endangered, the leopard is not at the point of extinction. But its close relative the tiger may soon become extinct in the wild.

If these sand eels are threatened, the puffin is also vulnerable.

## Not so cute

This puffin has a beakful of sand eels – small fish that it depends on for its food. Sand eels are not beautiful or glamorous, but without them puffins would find it difficult to survive. Today, sand eels are threatened by new and more efficient fishing techniques. To look after puffins, we have to look after their food sources too.

## Keeping count

Using an inflatable raft slung beneath a balloon, scientists survey treetop wildlife in a West African forest. Their work will show what lives in the trees, and how the numbers might be affected by changes to the environment. Many specimens collected in surveys like this are species that have never been seen before.

## Safety offshore

The tuatara is a unique lizard-like reptile that comes from New Zealand. It has been harmed by introduced species – particularly rats, which eat its eggs and its young. Today, tuataras survive only on about 30 small, offshore islands, where rats are kept under control.

Today's **extinction rate** **faster** than at any other time **since** the **dinosaurs disappeared**

# ACTION!
## SAVE ANIMALS

Never buy anything that has been made from tortoiseshell or wild animal fur.

If you are buying a pet, make sure it is one that has been bred in captivity, not caught in the wild.

Do not pay to watch performing animals that have been taken from the wild.

SINCE SHE WAS EIGHT YEARS OLD, STELLA NORCUP HAS DREAMED OF WORKING WITH APES. HER DREAM HAS COME TRUE AND SHE IS NOW A KEEPER-SCIENTIST AT Great Britain's Jersey Zoo, the international headquarters of the Durrell Wildlife Conservation Trust. Stella looks after a family of five western lowland gorillas.

**Ya Kwanza**
This male silverback is the leader of Jersey's gorilla troop. He was bred in captivity in Melbourne Zoo, Australia.

## A day in the life of an
# ANIMAL CONSERVATIONIST
Patient observation and careful animal management are needed if we are to save gorillas from extinction.

Wholemeal bread — Carrot — Apple — Lettuce — Green pepper

**Breakfast**
The first meal of the day includes some of the foods the gorillas might eat in the wild.

Fruit drink

**Liquid intake**
Healthy drinks, with vitamins, are prepared twice a day to maintain the gorillas' liquid intake.

**Today, Stella** will feed and check the health of the gorillas in her care at Jersey Zoo. She will also welcome visitors and help to raise their awareness of the urgent need for animal conservation.

**8:00am** Just like any other family, gorillas sometimes squabble or get sick. This is why my first job is to check that there are no obvious signs of sickness, such as diarrhea. Then I prepare breakfast while Ya Kwanza, the large male silverback, watches me. He is the leader of the group and 7 ft (2.1 m) tall

and 392 lb (178 kg) of pure muscle. Today he is not in a good mood. Hlala Kahilli, one of the females, and their playful son Mapema, who's just three and a half, are also watching.

**8:15am** The gorilla's diet is a low-calorie mixture of fruit, vegetables, and cereals. Breakfast includes wholemeal bread. I also feed each gorilla by hand and from a jug with a delicious mixture of milk, water, and fruit drink. The two other females are Kahilh and her daughter Sakina, who are last to be fed.

**8:30am** I open the doors and the family goes outside. It's time for the dirty part of the job – cleaning out the sleeping area. I remove the bedding, hose down the areas, and scrub the floors with vegetable-based detergent that will not harm the gorillas. I also collect any dung samples if they are needed to monitor the animals' health. All the waste is taken to our organic farm for "recycling" and is used as fertilizer to grow more food for the gorillas.

**Mucking out**
To keep them healthy, the gorillas' bedding is cleaned out and replaced every day.

**10:00am** Visitors start to arrive. I answer questions about our conservation work. It's important to make people aware that gorillas are an endangered species and are here for conservation reasons rather than for humans' entertainment. For every one gorilla alive on the planet, there are a million humans. I keep a constant watch to make sure people do not tease or feed the family. The gorillas cannot even eat natural food such as chestnuts, because their diet is so carefully balanced.

**10:30am** A member of our Conservation Education staff arrives with a group from a local school and talks about the gorilla's status in the wild. They also explain why we are breeding them in captivity. Then it's time to give the family something else to eat, but this time I scatter small items such as grapes or seeds on the ground. The gorillas have to forage for them among the grass and plants. This keeps them active because it is how they would have to search for their food in the wild.

Grapes form part of a gorilla's diet.

**11:15am** Now it's time to prepare the gorillas' lunch. This time it is a lighter meal that's made up from vegetables as well as edible plants, such as bamboo, which we grow around the enclosure.

**Jersey Zoo**
The mild climate is one reason why Gerald Durrell set up his zoo on Jersey, one of Great Britain's Channel Islands.

**12:00pm** Lunch is served. The gorillas are a close family unit and would live in a social group in the wild. Being together is what makes them happy. It's also important to make sure they have enough space and private areas in the enclosure so that they can get away from each other – or the public – if they want to. I always watch for signs that they are not happy with their surroundings.

**Feeding time**
Scatter feeds of small items encourage the gorillas to search for their food. They climb the netting for exercise.

**2:30pm** A second educational talk and scatter feed takes place. We emphasize to visitors that gorillas are wild animals. This is why we try to keep human contact to a minimum so that the gorillas act as naturally as possible and can be returned to the wild one day.

**4:00pm** Ya Kwanza and his family come inside for their evening meal. This time it includes a portion of yogurt, which we can use to hide the taste of medicine, and sunflower oil for glossy coats and healthy skin. If a gorilla is sick we call in one of our two vets. If it is serious, the gorilla may be taken to the zoo's fully equipped vet center.

Yogurt

Sunflower oil

**4:30pm** During the day I constantly monitor the gorillas' behavior to collect scientific data about how they live. I input all my observations into the computer. The data will help us to understand gorillas and prevent them from ever becoming extinct.

> **There's nothing in the world that can have the impact of coming in here and seeing a gorilla close by. They are ambassadors for gorillas in the wild.**

**Family ties**
Sakina watches her nephew, Mapema, as he waits patiently to see if she will share her food with him.

Mapema is in a playful mood as he knows dinner is on the way.

# LIVING
# CONDITIONS

THERE ARE NOW MORE THAN SIX
BILLION PEOPLE ON EARTH, AND THE
FIGURE IS RISING FAST. WE USE MORE OF THE
world's resources than ever before and produce an
ever-growing mountain of waste. To safeguard the
global environment, we need to learn how to use
less, and use it more effectively.

66 Ever-expanding consumption puts
strains on the environment – emissions
and wastes that pollute the Earth
and destroy ecosystems. 99

**UNITED NATIONS
HUMAN DEVELOPMENT REPORT 1998**

This tidy landscape in northern
France (main picture) seems a
world away from life in a big
city. But even in places like this,
wasteful lifestyles take their toll on
the environment. Most household
garbage is bulldozed into landfill
sites (inset), where it will be a
hazard for years to come.

# *People* PRESSURE

| | | |
|---|---|---|
| 1804 | 1 billion | |
| 1927 | 2 billion | |
| 1974 | 4 billion | |
| 1999 | 6 billion | |
| 2050 | | 10 billion |

## Population growth

The world's human population has been growing for thousands of years. But its steepest rise, shown in this chart, has happened in the last 100 years. Today, more than a quarter of a million babies are born every day.

**D**uring the past 100 years, something extraordinary has happened to the human race – our numbers have more than tripled. Improvements in hygiene, medicine, and food production are the reasons for this growth. There are now 6 billion people on the planet, and the total is still growing fast. This steep increase is good news in some ways. It shows that people are healthier than ever before. But the expanding human population also causes problems, because we use up more food, energy, and space every year. Improved family planning is one way in which population growth is now being brought under control.

" Travelers coming to Hong Kong often say that the city is a very wonderful place. However, for me, Hong Kong is a crowded, noisy place. So many people live here – it is hard to find any peace. When I sleep at night, my neighbors are always playing mahjong, and their stereo is turned up very loud. In the daytime, construction sites for new homes and office blocks near my school are always making a lot of noise with their machines. Bulldozers tear down walls and move earth, with lots of drillings and hammerings. Although we shut all the windows in our classroom, we can't hear what our teachers say in the lessons. Sometimes, I feel very frustrated about it. "   *Virginia Lau*

## Making space

As the world's population increases, more and more people are moving to cities to find work. It is not easy to make room for all these extra people. In Hong Kong, land has been reclaimed from the sea for office blocks and apartments, and a previously unspoiled coastline has been turned into an international airport.

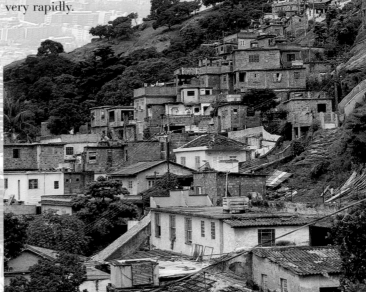

## The lure of cities

This shanty town, outside Rio de Janeiro, has been built by people who have moved from the countryside. Their houses do not have running water or proper drainage, and the result is pollution and disease. Scenes like this are common in countries where the population is growing very rapidly.

## Leaving the countryside

Here an empty farmhouse in France is surrounded by abandoned land. In the early 1900s, nine out of 10 people lived in the countryside. Today, only half the population leads a rural life. Population growth has caused people to move into cities in search of better-paid jobs. In some countries, so many people have moved that not enough remain to farm the land.

Although the **world's population** is **growing**, the **growth rate** has started to **fall**

## People on the move

A highway junction sprawls across the landscape in England. The larger the population, the more people there are traveling. This can mean more cars polluting the atmosphere, and more roads cutting through natural habitats. Using public transportation reduces the pollution as one vehicle can carry the same number of people as many cars.

**Population growth** is likely to **stop** at some time in the **21st century**

## The cost of travel

Everyone enjoys going on vacation – particularly to far-flung parts of the world. But air travel has a hidden cost, because it is a major source of atmospheric pollution. Air traffic has doubled in the last 15 years, and pollution from planes is an increasing problem. Although planes are becoming cleaner and more efficient all the time, plane pollution cannot be completely stopped.

# Wasteful

### Fatal attraction

For wild animals, our household waste can be life-threatening. Attracted by the smell of rotting food, this bear is exploring a garbage dump. It risks being injured by broken glass or by choking on discarded plastic.

**Plastic** is often **recyclable**, even though **most** of it gets **thrown away**

### Toxic time bomb

Industrial waste can be difficult to deal with because it is often poisonous. These chemical drums have broken open, which makes the problem even more serious. Because waste like this is expensive to dispose of safely, it may be dumped illegally.

**I**n nature, there is no such thing as waste because the material that living things produce gets broken down and reused. But in the human world, it is very different. Every year, each one of us produces up to three-quarters of a ton of household waste, adding to a growing mountain of garbage that has to find a home. But many of the items that we throw away are actually resources in disguise. Paper, glass, and metal can be recycled and reused, while kitchen and garden waste can be turned into compost that improves the fertility of the soil.

We need to **think** about ways to **reduce** the amount of **waste** we create

### Indecent burial

Surrounded by a garbage-strewn landscape, this bulldozer is spreading out household waste. When the site is full, the waste will be covered with soil, but it will have to be monitored for years to come. This is because waste produces inflammable gases and polluting sludge as it breaks down.

# World

## Compost from waste

At this processing plant in France, organic matter from household waste is being turned into compost that can be spread on fields. Organic matter makes up nearly a quarter of household garbage. It includes anything that comes from plants or animals, such as vegetable peelings and other leftover food.

## Dutch treatment

These recycling bins in the Netherlands have been color-coded according to their use – blue for paper, orange for textiles, green for glass, and yellow for cans. This speeds up the system of recycling and makes the whole process more energy efficient.

**Paper** can only be **recycled** up to 8 times before the fibers are **destroyed**

## Longer life

Household waste includes many different materials that can be recycled. Glass, for example, can be recycled forever because it never breaks down. Metal, as used for drink cans, can also be recycled indefinitely.

Glass can be used over and over again if it is taken for recycling.

## ACTION!
### REDUCE WASTE

Find out where your local recycling center is – and use it.

Take your lunch in a sandwich box rather than wrapping it in foil.

Use and refill your own drink bottle.

**GARBOLOGIST**
DR. BILL RATHJE

BILL RATHJE WAS TRAINED AS AN ARCHAEOLOGIST AND BECAME FASCINATED BY THE GARBAGE SOCIETIES LEAVE BEHIND. FROM THIS HE LEARNED HOW PEOPLE in the past had misused their environment. Today, his Garbage Project at the University of Arizona examines landfill sites to learn how to avoid repeating mistakes of the past.

**Landfill site**
This view shows Fresh Kills, Staten Island, the world's largest landfill site.

## A day in the life of a
# GARBOLOGIST

## By unearthing household trash we can learn better ways to dispose of it and save the Earth's resources.

**Today, Rathje** and his colleagues are digging garbage from a landfill site in New York. They hope to identify what our current civilization is throwing away. By discovering what damage is caused by today's waste, they can suggest ways to limit environmental damage.

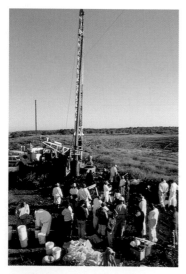

**Crew at work**
The landfill excavation crew at work around the bucket auger.

**4:00am** Arise and "suit-up" in our motel on Staten Island, New York City, just a couple of miles from the Fresh Kills site. Crew wear single-piece plastic overalls to protect from splashes, heavy boots with steel toes (and a steel plate in the sole), and heavy gloves. Later I may put on protective goggles and a face mask. Meet with my crew – Wilson Hughes, my codirector, and the six other members of the Project's "A-Team." Also with us are collectors of landfill samples, and three other crews that include microbiologists and solid waste management students.

**5:30am** After checking our equipment, we drive onto the landfill. There we meet up with Buddy Kellett, his crew, and the bucket auger – a mighty "road warrior" contraption that is used to drill 3-ft (1-m)-diameter cores of garbage out of the landfill so we can sort, weigh, measure, and record the contents. Wilson drives to the first drilling site and everyone follows along.

**Fresh garbage**
The bucket auger dumps a fresh load of garbage extracted from the landfill.

**Taking samples**
An assortment of the garbage crew at work on their sample-taking tasks.

**6:00am** After some grumbles of metal on metal, the driver pulls a lever and the graphite steel teeth around the bottom edge of the hollow bucket bite into the cover soil and the drilling begins. Bucket by bucket, landfill contents are brought to the surface and dumped onto a backdirt pile that will be used later to refill the hole that can become 100 ft (30 m) deep. About every 15 ft (4.5 m) the

driver swings the bucket out over our sampling board and dumps its contents. Researchers approach the pile of steaming garbage – ready to take its temperature, pull out swatches to test for microorganisms, and to shovel up a sample for detailed sorting back in the laboratory in Arizona. If the temperature of the garbage is high, we know that micro-organisms are organically breaking down (biodegrading) the landfill contents. Gavin Archer, one of the A-Team, will drive the samples to Arizona.

**Recording the evidence**
The garbage crew sorts and records the excavated refuse.

**10:00am** Just after we have moved to the second drilling site, two newspaper reporters and three TV news film crews show up for two hours of filming and interviews. I tell them that in previous digs we have discovered that all styrofoam, fast food packaging, and disposable diapers account for less than 3 percent of the space the garbage takes up in landfills.

We also learned that in "dry" landfills not much paper breaks down organically. The most unexpected discovery is that paper takes up 40–50 percent of the space in landfills. Despite the opportunities to recycle paper, the majority of people still don't do it. When a substance is described as biodegradable this really means it will break down as long as it is exposed to moisture and oxygen. These two conditions are not always present in a landfill site. Finally, I tell the media that we do not know what we will find in Fresh Kills – that's why we're digging here!

**Landfill site**
The map shows Staten Island, New York City, where Fresh Kills is located.

**Protective gloves**
Heavy-duty sorting gloves

**1:00pm** We break for lunch after the second well is filled. We brought sandwiches to the dig because the way we smell means we cannot go anywhere "public" to eat. Old garbage has a very distinctive aroma – but you get used to it.

**1:40pm** After lunch we start drilling again. I get "slimed" when the wind hits a bucket I am standing by as I help other crew members search through the backdirt pile for a newspaper that will date the excavated refuse. The slime is something new to us, and is due to the fact that Fresh Kills is a "wet" landfill at the bottom, which was once a tidal swamp.

**4:30pm** We finish the fourth and last well of the day – and backfill it so no one can fall in. Gavin drives the samples off to a storage area, and the rest of us head back to our motel. By 6 pm we're cleaned up and ready to eat. The laboratory crew will stay behind to culture their microbiological samples in the mobile lab. Our hope is that by understanding what is thrown away we can reduce damage to the environment in the future.

**On top of the pile**
Dr. Rathje stands among garbage at the end of a successful digging day.

**❝You need a poor sense of smell and a good sense of humor when studying the impact of garbage on the environment.❞**

**Dating system**
Crew sort through looking for newspapers that will date the garbage.

**Fine sorting**
Garbage samples are placed on the "mesh" and whatever falls through, called "fines," is sorted with tweezers and a magnifying glass.

The amount of **energy** used by the **human race** has **tripled** in just **40 years**

# Filthy

### Nuclear energy

Uranium fuel is lowered into the core of a nuclear reactor in France. Unlike power stations that burn fossil fuels, nuclear reactors do not produce any waste gases, so they do not pollute the air. However, uranium is a hazardous substance because it emits lethal radiation. Even after the fuel has been used, the radiation takes hundreds of years to fade away.

On average, **every person** on Earth **uses** the equivalent of **2 tons** of **coal** a **year**

## Each time you flip a switch, it is a reminder that modern life depends on energy. We use huge amounts of energy. Most of

it comes from burning fossil fuels, such as oil, coal, and gas, which are cheap and convenient. But fossil fuels create pollution when they are moved around, and even more when they are burned. Scientists are finding ways of reducing pollution by using fossil fuels more efficiently. We can prevent it entirely if we use clean energy, such as solar, wind, and water power.

### Gas on tap

Inching its way across the ground, this crane is laying a natural gas pipeline in Siberia. This kind of work can damage natural habitats, and it also opens up wilderness areas that used to be difficult for people to reach. However, natural gas does have one advantage – it contains very little sulphur, which makes it the cleanest burning fossil fuel.

### Mining coal

Huge amounts of rock have been cut away to reach the coal hidden below the ground in this Australian mine. Extracting coal is dangerous, and it also destroys natural habitats. When coal near the surface is dug up, trees and other plants are bulldozed away.

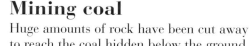

# FUEL

About **90** percent of the world's **crude** **oil** has **already** been **located**

## Drilling for oil

This pump is extracting oil from beneath the ground. At one time, oil was always drilled on land; but over the years, many land-based oil wells have run dry. Today, a large amount of the oil we use comes from wells drilled into the seabed. Oil pollutes the seabed by seeping out of wells, and it also kills coastal wildlife when tankers run aground.

Most of the energy used by the computer turns into waste heat.

## Generating electricity

Power stations generate the electricity we use at home, at school, and at work. Coal-fired power stations and their cooling towers, shown below, produce air pollution and waste heat. Modern gas-fired power stations are more efficient and also less polluting.

## Using electricity

When you use a computer, you may find it hard to believe that you are polluting the environment. Switching on a lamp, using the telephone, or turning on a fan could all have the same effect. All these appliances need electricity. This almost certainly comes from a power station that burns coal, gas, or oil, or from one that uses nuclear fuels.

When **fossil fuels** are **burned** to produce electricity, over **half** their **energy** is **lost** in **waste**

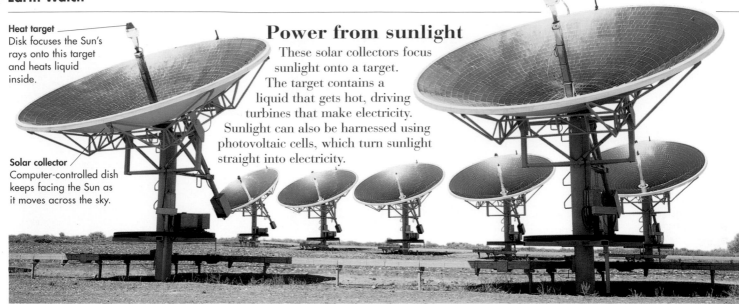

**Heat target**
Disk focuses the Sun's rays onto this target and heats liquid inside.

## Power from sunlight

These solar collectors focus sunlight onto a target. The target contains a liquid that gets hot, driving turbines that make electricity. Sunlight can also be harnessed using photovoltaic cells, which turn sunlight straight into electricity.

**Solar collector**
Computer-controlled dish keeps facing the Sun as it moves across the sky.

# A Cleaner Future

In a single day, enough solar energy falls on Earth to keep the human race going for more than 15 years. Unlike energy from fossil or nuclear fuels, this energy is self-renewing, and it causes no pollution. It keeps the planet warm, and it drives the currents that keep wind and water on the move. Today, only a tiny fraction of this energy is harnessed for human needs, mainly because it is too expensive. But technology is improving, and clean energy is becoming cheaper. Using clean energy could solve many of the world's pollution problems.

Screens keep house cool in summer.

Solar-powered lighting

### The energy-efficient house

This house in Vienna has been specially designed to use energy as efficiently as possible. Its windows let in lots of sunshine during the winter, but they keep most of it out in summer. The walls are well insulated so the temperature inside remains steady. Its hot-water supply is heated partly by solar power.

### Wind turbines

Wind power has only recently been used to generate electricity. Wind turbines like these might generate enough electricity to power a town. Although they are noisy and can spoil the view, they provide energy without producing any pollution.

## Water power

About one-fifth of all the electricity used in the world is generated by water. The water is held back by dams, like this one in Sri Lanka, and is piped downhill to drive turbines. This is called hydroelectric power.

## Dead end

Hydroelectric power is clean, but it can cause problems for water wildlife. The sockeye salmon is a fish that migrates up rivers to breed. It has been harmed by hydroelectric programs, because large dams stop it from reaching the places where it lays its eggs.

Insulated walls prevent house from losing heat to outside.

South-facing windows let sunshine in during the winter.

In theory, **wind** and **wave** power **could** generate **all** the **energy** that we **need**

In **Iceland**, four-fifths of the country's **homes** are **kept warm** by **geothermal** energy

## Energy from the Earth

At this power station in New Zealand, steam from hot rocks is used to drive turbines, producing pollution-free power. This clean source of power is known as geothermal energy. It uses heat from the interior of the Earth in places where this natural heat is not far below the surface.

## WATERWHEEL

EXPERIMENT

**You will need**: 2 thin plastic plates, Plasticine, a pair of compasses, 6 plastic can lids, double-sided adhesive tape, pencil, water, and basin.

**1 PLACE ONE PLATE** over a piece of Plasticine. Using the compasses, make a hole at the exact center, pushing the point into the Plasticine. Repeat with the second plate.

**2 USING THE TAPE,** stick the lids to the edge of one plate at six evenly spaced points. The lids should circle the plate, each one facing the bottom of the one in front.

**3 TAKE THE** second plate and, using the tape, stick it to the lids so it sits opposite the other plate. The lids are "sandwiched" between the two plates.

**4 PUSH THE** pencil through the holes in the plates. The waterwheel is complete. Hold it over a basin and let water run onto it from a faucet. As the water fills each lid, the wheel turns.

**This shows that:** by using a waterwheel, the energy in moving water can be converted into energy that can do useful work.

# Action Plan

IF YOU CARE ABOUT THE PLANET and want to help save its natural environment, there are many organizations that will help to get you involved. This list includes those you can contact in the US, as well as international organizations you can visit on the internet.

**Alaska Rainforest Campaign**
Coalition of groups working to protect the two remaining national forests in Alaska. The site has good links to other related organizations.

www.akrain.org

320 Fourth St, NE
Washington, DC 20002

**American Bird Conservancy**
Dedicated to the conservation of wild birds and their habitats. This website has information and campaigns about current issues such as the effect of climate change on birds.

www.abcbirds.org

PO Box 249
The Plains, VA 20198

**American Society for the Prevention of Cruelty to Animals (ASPCA)**
National charity involved in all aspects of animal welfare. The site has a kid's section with information and ideas for school projects.

www.aspca.org

424 East 92nd St
The Plains, VA 20198

**British Antarctic Survey**
An organization responsible for the UK's scientific research in Antarctica and the Southern Ocean. The BAS website gives full details of research programs currently underway.

www.antarctic.ac.uk

High Cross
Madingley Road
Cambridge CB3 0ET
UK

**Care for the Wild**
A wildlife charity that protects animals from cruelty and exploitation. Based in the UK, but also supports work to help endangered species worldwide.

www.careforthewild.org

1 Ashfolds
Horsham Road
Rusper
West Sussex RH12 4QX
UK

**Coastal Rainforest Coalition**
Dedicated to protecting the rain forests of British Columbia by promoting ecologically sound alternatives.

www.coastalrainforest.org

2180 Dwight Way
Berkeley, CA 94704

**Earthwatch Institute**
An international organization that promotes conservation by funding education and expeditions, sometimes to remote parts of the world.

www.earthwatch.org

3 Clock Tower Place, Suite 100
Box 75
Maynard, MA 01754

**Environmental Investigation Agency**
An international campaigning organization committed to improving conservation laws – and making sure that existing laws are upheld. EIA agents work worldwide, often undercover.

www.eia-international.org

69 Old Street
London EC1V 9HX
UK

**Environmental Protection Agency**
A US government agency that works to safeguard the environment and protect human health. Visit the EPA website for information on a wide range of environmental topics, including details about global warming.

www.epa.gov

**Friends of the Earth**
An international network of environmental groups that commissions research and campaigns for changes in the law.

www.foei.org

1025 Vermont Ave NW
3rd floor
Washington, DC 20005-6303

**Greenpeace**
One of the world's leading environmental organizations, involved in direct action to safeguard the planet's future.

www.greenpeace.org

Canonbury Villas
London N1 2PN
UK

**International Wildlife Coalition**
An international conservation organization with an award-winning website. Visit it to see the news desk and the monthly endangered species watch.

www.iwc.org

70 East Falmouth Highway
East Falmouth, MA 02536

**National Audubon Society**
With more than half a million members, the NAS is one of the foremost US conservation organizations.

www.audubon.org

700 Broadway
New York, NY 10003

**Rainforest Alliance**
A US-based organization that supports rain forest conservation and also runs programs that identify environmentally friendly products.

www.rainforest-alliance.org

65 Bleecker Street
New York, NY 10012

**Rainforest Concern**
An organization that identifies and protects threatened areas of tropical rainforest, particularly in areas of South America.

www.rainforest.org.uk

27 Lansdowne Crescent
London W11 2NS
UK

**Royal Society for the Protection of Birds**
Europe's largest conservation charity, with more than a million members. The RSPB helps to conserve wild birds and their habitats.

www.rspb.org.uk

The Lodge
Sandy
Bedfordshire SG19 2DL
UK

**Sea Shepherd Conservation Society**
An organization devoted to conserving and protecting life in the oceans. Has its own fleet of boats which investigate illegal fishing and whaling.

www.seashepherd.org

PO Box 2616
Friday Harbor, WA 98250

**Sierra Club**
One of the leading US environmental organizations. The Sierra Club campaigns to protect wildlife, wilderness, and unspoiled habitats.

www.sierraclub.org

85 Second Street, Second Floor
San Francisco, CA 94105-5500

**Soil Association**
Based in the UK, one of the first organizations to campaign for organic agriculture and against intensive farming.

www.soilassociation.org

Bristol House
40-56 Victoria Street
Bristol
Avon BS1 6BY
UK

**Whale and Dolphin Conservation Society**
A UK-based charity that campaigns for the protection of whales, dolphins, and porpoises around the world.

www.wdcs.org

Alexander House
James St. West
Bath BA1 2BT
UK

**Wildlife Preservation Society of Australia**
Founded in 1909, the WPSA campaigns to protect Australia's unique wildlife, which is often endangered by species introduced from other parts of the world.

nccnsw.org.au/member/wps

GPO Box 3428
Sydney, NSW 1043
Australia

**Willing Workers on Organic Farms (WWOOF)**
An international organization that helps people find out about short working breaks on organic farms.

www.phdcc.com/wwoof/wpusa

**World Conservation Monitoring Center**
A unique website that gives visitors a chance to find out about the world's endangered animals. Enter the name of any species, and the site will tell you if it is under threat.

www.wcmc.org.uk/species/animals

219 Huntingdon Road
Cambridge CB3 0DL
UK

**Worldwide Fund for Nature (WWF)**
The world's largest international conservation organization. Visit the website to find out about WWF and to check out the Living Planet Report.

www.panda.org

1250 24th St NW
PO Box 97180
Washington, DC
20037-1175

# Index

# Credits

**Dorling Kindersley would like to thank:**
Sheila Hanly for locating many of the Day in the Life experts; Amanda Carroll, Sheila Collins, Sharon Grant, Claire Legemah, Keith Newell, Peter Radcliffe, and Laura Roberts for design help; Lynn Bresler, index.

Andy Crawford for photography of the experiments, and models Harriet Couchman and Dejaune Davis.

Thanks also to Day in the Life experts and their organizations who provided many of the photographs: David Vaughan (Glaciologist), Jonathan Denison (Hydrologist), Larraine Yeagar (Organic Farmer), Stella Norcup/Jersey Zoo (Animal Conservationist), and Bill Rathje (Garbologist).

Special photography: Peter Anderson, Paul Bricknell, Geoff Brightling, Jane Burton, Philip Dowell, Frank Greenaway, Colin Keates, Dave King, Cyril Laubscher, Bill Ling, Ian O'Leary, Jim Robbins, Tim Ridley, Karl Shone, Kim Taylor, James Stevenson, Stephen Whitehorn, Alex Wilson, Jerry Young. Artwork: Kenneth Lilly, Martin Kamm. Models: Matthew Ward.

**Picture Credits**
*The publishers would like to thank the following for their kind permission to reproduce the photographs:*
a = above; c = center; b = bottom; l = left; r = right; t = top; f = far; n = near.

**Austin Brown/Aviation Picture Library:** 24tcr. **British Antarctic Survey:** 16tl, 16bl, 16br, 16-17t, 17tr, 17bc. **Bruce Coleman Ltd:** David Austen 54bl; Gerald S Cubitt 36bl, 39cr; John Cancalosi 37tl, 57bc; Mark Boulton 19tl. **Colorific!:** James Sugar / Black Star 31tr; Steve Shelton / Black Star 23br. **Julian Cotton Photo Library: 14tc,** 48-9, 56t. **Sue Cunningham Photographic:** 43tr. **Environmental Images:** Dominic Sansoni 57tc; Herbert Girardet 29c, 56-7cb; Irene Lengui 49tr; John Arnould 36-7bc; Leslie Garland 18br; Robert Brock 50c; Robert Brook 27c; Steve Morgan 15bl. **Eye Ubiquitous:** Bennett Dean 33tr. **Fauna & Flora International:** 39tr. **The Garbology Project, University of Arizona:** 52tl, 52cr, 52bl, 52br, 52-3l, 53cl, 53b; Louie Psihoyos 53cr. **Robert Harding Picture Library:** 49br. **Holt Studios International:** Inga Spence 33cl, 33br; Nigel Cattlin 32cl. **Hutchison Library:** Jeremy A Horner 32bc; Mary Jelliffe 21tl. **Impact Photos:** Gerald Buthaud / Cosmos 40bc. **FLPA - Images of Nature:** David Hosking 41br. **N.A.S.A.:** Finley Holiday Films 4-5. **Natural History Museum, London:** 13bl. **Nature Photographers:** 21tr. **N.H.P.A.:** David E Myers 13tl. **Oxford Scientific Films:** G I Bernard 35cr; Michael Fogden 15tr; Tim Jackson 14br. **Panos Pictures:** 25tl; Fred Hoogervest 25tr; Marc Schlossman 25b. **Planet Earth Pictures:** David A Ponton 14tr; Doug Perrine 37tr; John Downer 37br; Jonathan Scott 36c; Richard Matthews 43c; Robert A Jureit 38tr. **Rex Features:** Alexandra Boulant 51tl, 51tr. **Science Photo Library:** Catherine Pouedras 54tl; Eye of Science 13tcr; G Jacobs, Stennis Space Centre 22-23tc; Jeff Lepore 40tl; Kaj R Svensson 31tl; Martin Bond 33tc; Michael Marten 46; Michael Martin 7tr; Sabine Weiss 30bc; T Stevens & P McKinley, Pacific Northwest Laboratory 13bc; Tom McHugh 19c; Weiss, Jerrican 19b. **Still Pictures:** Adrian Arbib 22bl; Fritz Polking 24tr; Joe St Leger 40-41; John Maier 26bl; John Paul Kay 32t; Klein / Hubert 40br; M & C Denis-Huot 41cr; Mark Edwards 31c; Norbert Wu 37cl. **Tony Stone Images:** 2-3 Endpapers, 67t, 43cl, 62-3 Endpapers; Ben Osborne 27t; Billy Hustace 52bc; Bob Kinst 6tl; Bob Krist 10; Bryan Mullenix 20-2l; Charles Krebs 15tl; David Meunch 12tl; David Muench 12tl; David Woodfall 26-7c, 47; Ed Pritchard 18tl, 49c; Frans Lanting 39tl; Jacques Jangoux 38-39b, 58-9; James Randhlev 37tc; Jeremy Walker 54-55b; John Lamb 48-9bj; Johnny Johnson 57cl; Keren Su 42bl; Larry Goldstein 9-10b; Martin Puddy 22-23c; Michael Javorka 28-29t; Nick Vedros 50-51b; Sandra Baker 55cl. **Topham Picturepoint:** 54cr; UNEP/Daniel Frank 49tl.

**Jacket Credits**
**Bruce Coleman Ltd:** Bob & Clara Calhoun front c; Dr Eckart Pott front bl. **Julian Cotton Photo Library:** back cb. **Science Photo Library:** G Jacobs, Stennis Space Centre, Geosphere Project back tl; Sabine Weiss front br. **Tony Stone Images:** David Meunch back cra; Keren Su front bc & back bl; Martin Puddy front inside flap b.